A Hundred Years of Carfin Grotto

John Watts

MUNGO

Glasgow

2022

This book does not attempt to emulate the excellent accounts of the Carfin Grotto already written by Mgr Taylor, Susan McGhee and, more recently, Frank Devlin. They were far better qualified than I for the task, and anyone who has read their works will easily see the extent of my debt to them.

Nor does the present volume offer a Guide to the Grotto, for an attractive and useful one is already in print and available.

Instead, it tells the story year by year from 1922 to today in words and pictures, the text explaining the images and the images illustrating the text. It includes an Introduction mapping the circumstances that led to the Grotto's founding, and an Afterword offering some brief reflections on it.

The need to produce a book at an affordable price set a limit on its length, so that inevitably some events and some names have had to be omitted. It is hoped nonetheless that there is plenty in its pages to interest and inform, and that as such it may make a modest contribution to the Grotto's Centenary celebrations.

As well as the written works referred to above, I have made extensive use of a number of first-hand sources, including contemporary newspaper accounts. As to the images, most of those in the first two thirds of the book are taken from the Carfin Archive, which offers a rich resource for the Grotto's earlier years. For the more recent era, photographs and advice

have been kindly provided by a number of people, and I wish to thank very gratefully the following particularly for their ready and generous help: Fr Gerard Bogan (St Columba's, Viewpark), Fr Michael Briody (St Michael's, Moodiesburn), Hugh Buchanan, Derek Burns, Maureen Burns, Michael Burns, Kevin Cameron, James Connelly, Elodie Depierrepont (Office Central de Lisieux), Tom Eadie, Benedetta Guarrancino (The Catholic Herald), Daniel Harkins (Scottish Catholic Observer), Jim Hoey, Mike Hughes, Tommy and Thomas Hughes, Donna Maguire (Scottish Catholic Archives), Dr Mary McHugh (Glasgow Diocesan Archives), Brian Timmons & John P Mallon (Sancta Familia Media), Paul McSherry, Mgr Thomas Millar (Parish Priest at Carfin and Guardian [Administrator] of the Grotto 2002–11), Sr Rosemary Reilly and Clair Sweeney (Aid to the Church in Need). I am especially grateful to Fr Bogan, Fr Briody, Hugh Buchanan and James Connelly for kindly reading the draft text and for their valuable suggestions.

Warm thanks also to our sons Pádraig and Caoimhín for technical help with the photographs, and to Colin Hughes and Thomas Davie of Mungo Books for their excellent production.

Lastly, my gratitude to Bishop Joseph Toal, and to Fr James Grant (Guardian of the Grotto) and Fr Francis McGachey (Guardian 2011–2019), for their encouragement, help and generous support.

Frontispiece: Fr Taylor pictured around 1908 (see page 5), Carfin Archive
Left: Carfin parishioners on the 1920 pilgrimage to Lourdes (see page 7), Carfin Archive

The village of Carfin lies in the heart of the Lanarkshire coalfield, some 13 miles south-east of Glasgow and 2.5 north-east of Motherwell. Its days as a village really began in the mid-nineteenth century with the opening of pits in the neighbourhood. At that time it must have looked much like the other villages nearby – single-storey miners' rows, mainly 'single ends' or 'but and bens' of darkened sandstone.

Most of the villagers hailed originally from Ulster, and particularly Donegal. Their Irish origins were reflected in the names of the local football teams, the Carfin Hibernian and the Shamrock.

Three-quarters of the village were Catholic. Their spiritual needs were at first served from St Ignatius', Wishaw, the only parish in that whole area of North Lanarkshire. But in 1862 the Wishaw priest opened a Mass centre in the village, and soon after built a school-chapel there. In 1875 Carfin became a parish in its own right.

Parishes were also opening in neighbouring villages at this time, but Carfin continued to serve not only its own community but also Newarthill, New Stevenston, Cleekhimin, and (until 1890) Cleland. In 1882 the parish got its own church at last – a fine Pugin building able to hold 700 people – and fourteen years later a large new school was opened on the same site. In 1900 the parish priest Fr Webb purchased an acre of waste ground across the road from the church, an acquisition that was to play a crucial part in our story.

Thomas Nimmo Taylor was born in 1873 in Greenock, where his father was headteacher at St Lawrence's parish school. He himself began his own education at the local convent school run by the Franciscan Sisters, from whom he learned a love of St Francis that was to last throughout his life (in his twenties he became a Franciscan Tertiary).

At seventeen he began training for the priesthood. After a year in Scotland he entered the seminary of St Sulpice in France, where he spent the whole of his formation and was ordained by the Archbishop of Paris in 1897. His years in the particular late nineteenth century religious environment of France and St Sulpice – with its traditions of particular love of the Blessed Virgin and of visible and communal expressions of Faith, for example – played a key part in his own spiritual formation.

Returning to Scotland, he served as a curate in St Patrick's, Dumbarton until 1900 when he was appointed Professor at the senior seminary, St Peter's College, a post he held for the next fifteen years (the frontispiece photo dates from this time). Here again, he encountered a 'continental' experience. There were a number of students from the Rhineland in the college at the time, as well as several Belgian priests on the staff, one of whom, Fr Octavius Claeys, was to become a lifelong friend. Through Fr Claeys especially he was introduced to the tradition of public religious processions, notably the annual procession of the Precious Blood in Bruges. We have his own word that it was his friend who first planted the idea of processions which were later to become such a feature of the Carfin Grotto. And the Belgian priest was to be influential in other ways too, as we shall see.

Already at St Peter's Fr Taylor was showing the signs of becoming a very exceptional priest: a man of deep commitment to his Faith, and a passion to share it with others; a charismatic man, in both the religious and popular senses of the word; small of frame but great of heart; learned, yet simple and frugal; driven and indefatigable.

His priestly priorities were many, but perhaps the most important were the following. In the first place, he saw himself as essentially a missionary priest. Having twice unsuccessfully sought to join the foreign missions, he made Scotland his mission field. His zeal in bringing others to Christ was reflected in his own priestly motto (which he took from Francis Xavier, the patron saint of missionaries) – 'Jésus et les âmes'. He continued to support the foreign missions throughout his life, and indeed for some years served as Scottish President of the Pontifical Societies for Missions.

He was a man of prayer, which he called the key to God's treasury. Use it, he urged a friend, 'not a dozen but a thousand times daily'. He himself, one might almost say, made his whole life a prayer.

He had a deep love of the Blessed Sacrament. In the words of his biographer, it was 'the lodestar of his sacerdotal life'. He joined the Eucharistic League and the Priests' Eucharistic League as a young man, in time rising to a high position in both. His work of promoting the Eucharist was greatly helped when in 1905 Pius X recommended its regular reception by the faithful, and introduced Communion for teenagers and children.

The young and their spiritual welfare were a special concern for him in fact (and we can perhaps discern his father's influence in this). He loved to help them, and loved especially their innocence. While at St Peter's he was appointed Scottish Director of the Holy Childhood, an office he was to fulfil energetically for many years.

At the heart of his spiritual life was a deep devotion to the Blessed Virgin, and to her Rosary. His love of her had been given a particular focus in 1893, during his time at St Sulpice, when he and a fellow student paid a visit to the Marian shrine at Lourdes. At that time Lourdes was barely known in Scotland, and he was one its very first Scottish pilgrims. Soon his visits were to become almost annual, his last one made more than sixty years after the first.

It was probably at St Peter's that he read about a replica of Lourdes that had opened in the Ghent suburb of Oostacker in Belgium in 1873. No doubt he discovered more about it from Fr Claeys. What particularly touched his imagination was the extraordinary cure of a man's diseased and useless leg at the shrine. Perhaps the embryo of an idea for something similar in Scotland was already forming in his mind, for as he wrote later, 'it was Oostacker that suggested [a] Scottish Lourdes'.

It was when returning from a visit to Rome in 1903 that he called on the Carmel at Lisieux in Normandy. Having that year read the life story of Sœur Thérèse Martin he wanted to see for himself the Carmel that she had entered at age fifteen and where she had remained until her untimely death a mere nine years later. While there he suggested that the Order should seek to introduce her Cause. The visit was to be for him the beginning of a lifelong devotion to the Little Flower and a close association with the Carmelite community at Lisieux. He would in time become the leading promoter of Thérèse's Cause in the English-speaking world. In 1904 he wrote a short biography of her, and later he translated and published her own autobiography. The two books, which both achieved six figure sales, did much to make her a household name in Britain and America. In 1911 he was called as a witness at the Vatican's investigation of her Cause for sainthood.

In 1915 Fr Taylor was appointed parish priest of St Francis Xavier's, Carfin. Significantly, one of his first initiatives the following year was to organise a Corpus Christi procession in the church grounds; from 1921 this took place in the village streets. In 1920 he led a parish group on the Scottish National Pilgrimage to Lourdes (see photo on page 2). On their return the party, fired by their experience and no doubt prompted by their priest, took the decision to build a replica Lourdes Grotto as well as an Institute or hall on the acre of waste ground that Fr Webb had bought for the parish. On the advice of their archbishop the Grotto was originally intended to be a modest one for the parish – there was certainly no thought of a national shrine at this stage.

The work began that September. The Institute was completed by the following February, the rubble dug up in the laying of its foundations being put to use to help build the 'hill' of the Grotto. The spadework was carried out almost entirely by volunteer miners from the village, helped by others from Cleland and elsewhere, all of whom were idle that year due to the prolonged national Miners' Strike. Not only did this make the building possible, it was also in Fr Taylor's mind that working for such a good cause would ease the men's boredom and greatly help their sense of purpose and morale.

The miners responded magnificently. Nonetheless, as the winter of 1921–2 deepened and the working conditions became nigh impossible, the volunteers gradually dropped away until only a single man remained. Fr Taylor's response was to hold a novena to the Little Flower and place her relic on the boundary of the site. The very next Monday the volunteers were back, and the project was completed by the end of summer.

The parish curate, Fr John J. Murphy (who was to be Fr Taylor's invaluable assistant in the early days of the Grotto), had been sent to Oostacker to examine the shrine there. He had seen the 'stream' of running water that had been plumbed in, imitating the natural one at Lourdes, and at his suggestion a similar arrangement was made at Carfin by piping water from the mains. The rocky hill was beautified with flowers and shrubs, and a piece of rock from Lourdes was placed in it, set in a slab of Iona marble. Life-size statues of Mary and a kneeling Bernadette, made in Rome of Carrara marble and donated by local bookmaker and ex-miner Patrick Nugent, completed the work. Their arrival from Italy was delayed, but it turned out to be a happy delay, for the revised date of opening was a most auspicious one, Sunday 1 October, the feast of Our Lady of the Rosary.

Unlike some of the world's famous shrines, the Carfin Grotto had not come about following an apparition, or a message. It began with a decision to build a replica. And the decision was a group one. Nonetheless, there is no doubt that Fr Taylor was the driving force behind it, just as he would be of its growth over the next forty years. And with hindsight we can see that a number of circumstances had come together to create it. Fr Taylor's own temperament and experiences – his particular spiritual development and religious interests, the people, places and events that he encountered along the way, the mining parish that he came to serve – all these made fertile soil for germinating the idea of a Marian shrine in Scotland. They were the roads that led to the Grotto. And as we shall see, they would also to a large extent inform the special and unique character that it was to develop as it grew.

On 1 October 1922, the Grotto was dedicated and blessed by Fr Taylor, assisted by his curate Fr Murphy and five other priests, before a crowd of 2000 (1). The photograph shows the shrine as it was originally constructed – simple, with short steps up to two niches, in the right one of which is Fr Taylor. The ceremony was conducted by the parish priest rather than by a more senior figure in the Church, because at this time the Grotto was seen as a parish shrine only.

Image 2 was taken in the late spring of 1923, and shows devotees including a mother and her children praying before the shrine. The Institute can just be seen in the background. Private devotion by all ages was already an established practice by this date.

The Vatican's Investigation of the Cause of Thérèse Martin (3) had moved swiftly to her beatification in April 1923. Fr Taylor attended the official Declaration in Rome, and on his return set up a small statue of Blessed Thérèse in the Grotto.

His action met with disapproval from some in the Scottish Church – a 'storm of protest' he called it – who thought that a shrine to the Little Flower might detract from the Grotto's main purpose, devotion to the Virgin Mary. That summer he visited Lisieux and discussed the matter with Thérèse's sisters. They were certain that the effect would in fact be the opposite, and that the statue should stay. 'Keep the statue in the Grotto!' her sister Pauline the prioress urged; 'we shall ask our Thérèse to draw souls to Carfin and so prove how she loves Our Lady'. Their advice was followed, and their prediction amply confirmed – by October some 250,000 pilgrims had visited the Grotto.

Thus the decision to introduce the Little Flower was proved justified. Indeed, with hindsight we can see that her presence, and her beatification (and subsequent canonisation two years later) fell most providentially for the infant Grotto, and played a key part in its astonishing growth in popularity.

In January 1924 the Archbishop of Glasgow Donald Mackintosh visited the Grotto (**4**).* Seeing for himself the great numbers of visitors that it attracted, he readily agreed with Fr Taylor's argument for the need to enlarge the site, and gave permission for a semi-circular embankment to be added with a three-step terrace, for new steps and walkways on the hill with a 'pulpit' above the statue of Mary, and for the replacement of the Institute by a larger one. The work began at once, and enough was completed to allow the shrine to be re-opened for Easter.

* Until 1947 the area (including Carfin) that now comprises the Diocese of Motherwell was part of the Archdiocese of Glasgow.

That summer the police informed Fr Taylor that the parish Corpus Christi procession could not be held in the street as before, since the wearing of Catholic vestments in public was illegal under an Act of 1829. The event was therefore switched to the Grotto grounds (**5**).

4

5

Word of the ban came via the Knights of St Columba to Francis Blundell, MP for Ormskirk and himself a Grand Knight. Blundell raised the issue in Parliament, arguing that the old Act should be repealed as a matter of justice and that the Catholics of Scotland were entitled to equality and would accept nothing less. Despite opposition from several members, notably local Motherwell MP Hugh Ferguson (the man behind the ban), the Act was replaced by a new Roman Catholic Relief Act in 1926 that abolished the last remaining vestiges of discrimination. Thus it was that the banning of a procession in distant Carfin had led directly to every Catholic in Britain enjoying equal rights in law for the first time in three and a half centuries.

5

Fr Taylor had the greatest admiration for his volunteer builders, 'the Crusaders' as he called them. Only those who had seen them at work, he wrote, in all weathers and at all hours, could appreciate what they had achieved. Photo **6**, probably taken in February 1924, shows them bringing earth up to create the embankment. There were 300 volunteers in all, with some three dozen men working on this part of the project at any one time.

Image 7 shows other volunteers demolishing the first Institute. Some of those assisting them are mere boys. In this and the previous photograph the gangs have stopped work to 'stand still for the camera' to prevent a blurred image, and have taken up suitable poses.

In photo 8 a large contingent of the Crusaders have been brought together for a formal photograph with Fr Taylor, with the parish church and school in the background. Perhaps some readers can spot a grandad or great-uncle on these pages?

6

9

10

18

11

On the opposite page are two early photographs of visitors to the Grotto. Photo 9 shows a crowd waiting to fill up cups from the pool which was fed by the piped water 'stream'. In 10 a party of parishioners from St Mary's, Calton are walking in procession from Holytown station: the men are in the front, all are dressed in their Sunday best and reciting the Rosary as they go.

On 24 July 1924 the English Cardinal Bourne visited Carfin, driving through decorated streets in an open landau to the Grotto, where he preached to a crowd estimated at up to 50,000 (11). He called Carfin 'the gathering place of faithful hearts', and suggested that God had chosen it, just as He had chosen Nazareth, and Lourdes and Fatima, because it was a humble community. Behind him can be seen the new 'Lourdes Institute' nearing completion. Built on two storeys, its most prominent facility was the large tea room upstairs, that featured a stage and could double as a hall for concerts and pageants. It was completed that November, at a total cost of £6000.

PROPOSED VOTIVE CHURCH
OF OUR LADY, CARFIN

12

20

PROPOSED VOTIVE CHURCH
OF CHRIST.

The parish church was now clearly inadequate to cope with the crowds of visitors, and Archbishop Mackintosh gave permission for a new votive church to be built once all other debts had been cleared. A further five acres of land had been acquired, including the hill known as 'Maryknoll' above the Grotto, and it was here that the church was to be sited. The architect Reginald Fairlie, designer of a number of fine Catholic Churches at this time and responsible for the National Library of Scotland in Edinburgh, was engaged to design a great building large enough to accommodate 6000 (**12**), as well as an open court able to hold 30,000, bounded by a cloistered walkway and with an altar for the outdoor celebration of Mass (**13**). Majestic in scale and style and visible from afar atop its hill, one can imagine the impression it would have made upon the North Lanarkshire landscape.

To the end of his days Fr Taylor cherished the hope that the project might be realised.

Photo 14 was taken in early spring 1924, when work had started on enhancing the Grotto. Bernadette has now been raised from her original position at ground level, to make her visible even from the back of a large gathering; also in the picture are the electric lights installed the previous year to allow events to be held after dark.

15

Photograph 15 from summer 1925 shows the project now finished, with steps and paths, the pulpit and the new Institute. Note the 'rocks' above the shrine, some painted white, which were in fact slag from local mine workings.

At about this time a further forty acres of land were added to the Grotto.

In May 1925 Blessed Thérèse was canonised. The previous year her modest statue in the Grotto had been replaced by a larger one of Carrara marble. Mounted on a plinth it stood sixteen feet above ground level (**16**), and could be seen even by the largest crowd on the 'Little Flower Terrace' in front of it, where there was space for 15,000 pilgrims.

The new saint's feast day, 3 October (today her feast day is 1 October.) almost coincided with the Grotto's own anniversary, and was made the occasion for a double celebration. Because Thérèse had promised that after her death she would shower roses from heaven upon those who sought her help, now roses were blessed for the pilgrims. From 1927 the tradition began on 'Little Flower Sunday' of thousands of artificial roses, prepared by the parishioners, being handed out to the crowd who held them up to be blessed, as in photo **17** (see also page 41).

From May–July 1926 Fr Taylor was on a fund raising tour of the USA, where he was introduced to President Coolidge at the White House. At home the men of the parish again had time on their hands during the six months long Miners' Strike, and they used it to lay lawns, paths and shrubberies at the Grotto, working a morning or afternoon shift, at the end of which they each received a packet of cigarettes.

May 1927 saw the first Children's Day at the Grotto. Most parishes ran organisations for young people at this time, among them the Boy Scouts and Cubs and the Boys' Guild, and for girls the Guides and the Children of Mary. In summer 1927 all these groups held their own gatherings at the Grotto for the first time. Photo **18** shows the Archdiocesan Guides in procession, and **19** a troop of Cubs in the front of a crowd.

19

In image 20 the girls in white costumes are taking part in a Children of Mary pageant. The Boys' Guild also held their first rally this year. All these gatherings were to become annual events.

21

The year 1927 was in fact something of an
annus mirabilis for the Grotto. Not only did
these youth groups and other organisations
hold events for the first time; there was also
extraordinary activity in the creation of new
shrines. The idea for this apparently came
from Mgr Claeys: he argued that more shrines
would hold the interest of visitors who often
travelled to Carfin from afar and would wish
to make a day of it. Thus began a development
that has continued till today, and which is almost unique to Carfin.

First of the new shrines was that of St Anne,
the mother of Mary, donated by the people of
Quebec and opened in May (**21**).

A second new shrine from the same year was the Calvary (**22**). The impressive 24ft cross, rough hewn from a larch trunk, was donated by a local coal master, while the bronze figures of Mary, St John and St Mary Magdalene were cast in Tourcoing in northern France.

Unfortunately, the wood of the cross was later found to be diseased and had to be replaced with another less striking but more lasting. The ground upon which it was set was also greatly built up to create a 'Calvary Hill' (**23**). Photo **24** shows the shrine as it is today.

23

24

In May-June of the same year a hundred volunteers completed the huge task of creating a lake at the Grotto, with an island on which to set the newly acquired statue of Stella Maris (Our Lady Star of the Sea). The new shrine was dedicated in July. Image **25** shows it as it looked when first completed.

The following year the bed of the lake was treated to prevent leakage, and the island was heightened, turfed and planted with shrubs, as in Photo **26**, which also offers a good view of part of the shamrock-shaped 'sea', and the new two arched stone bridge linking Mary's island with the 'mainland' (see also page 92).

Other new shrines in 1927 were those of St Joseph, and St Joachim the father of Mary. But perhaps the most important addition that year was the opening by the LMS (the London, Midland & Scottish Railway Co.) of a station close by, the 'Carfin Grotto Halt', to cater for the ever growing number of pilgrims.

27

The final statue commissioned in 1927 was that of Christ the King, a devotion being promoted at this time by Pius XI. Like most of the others up to the Second World War, it was carved in Italy from Carrara marble at the Bresciani School at Capezzano. The statue is of heroic size and majesty, so heavy that the cost of transportation delayed its arrival until just before Christmas, forcing the dedication to be postponed to January 1928.

Photo **27** was taken that month, the winter trees emphasising the bareness of this part of the Grotto. Image **28**, taken in summer, shows some of the biblical inscriptions around the pedestal proclaiming the kingship of Jesus. How different the view today (**29**)! The shrine is now far less massive, since much of the base has been discarded, and the background is utterly changed.

34

28

29

In 1928 a statue of St Anthony was gifted to the Grotto by a parishioner of St Anthony's, Govan in memory of two deceased brothers of Fr Taylor who had associations with that parish, one as a curate, the other as a teacher in the school. The land where the shrine was sited was marshy, and when in 1929 the Glasgow Franciscan Third Order (TOSF) donated a statue of St Francis to the Grotto, the area was covered with a hill of earth on which to set the two saints. St Anthony was placed near the summit of this 'Mount Assisi' with a lamb beside him, from where a spring of water flowed down through seven pools symbolising the seven Sacraments and the River of the Water of Life that flows from the Lamb in the Book of Revelation (**30**).

The first national pilgrimage of the TOSF, held that September, was made the occasion for the blessing of the completed Franciscan shrine. A statue of St Francis was carried into the Grotto by the Tertiaries in procession (**31** opposite) after which the shrine was blessed by Fr Herbert OFM, the Guardian of the Glasgow Friary (**32**).

31

32

Image 33 gives an overall view of Mount Assisi soon after its completion. The tall figure of St Anthony breaks the skyline at the summit, with Francis at the foot of the hill near the pilgrim path, as befits the 'Little Poor Man' who was the humblest of saints and always close to the people.

That same year saw the building of the 'Bethlehem Cave' (**34**), appropriately sited beside Mount Assisi since it was St Francis who began the now worldwide tradition of the Christmas Crib. The Cave and its figures and star window were designed by the family firm of Gerard Dupon of Bruges, whose different members were skilled in painting, sculpture and stained glass. M Dupon, who was introduced to Fr Taylor by Mgr Claeys, became his friend and artistic adviser; his firm created many of the Grotto's treasures in the inter-war years (see further pages 46–7, 52, 74–5, 98 and 107).

34

Children were not only encouraged to attend the Grotto's pageants and other events, they were given prominent parts to play in them. So for example on Mission Sunday, one of Fr Taylor's favourite days, some had their faces painted – brown or yellow or black – in order to play the part of children from the different mission lands. And in many of the processions a contingent always accompanied the adults. Photo **35** shows boys in one such procession.

36

Among the most colourful pageants were those held on Little Flower Sunday at the beginning of October, and Rosary Sunday in August. The first featured a young parishioner dressed as St Thérèse (**36**), accompanied by her attendants. From 1927 the pageant featured the Blessing of Roses, which were distributed to the crowd, while the procession, held after dark beneath hanging coloured lights, included a relic of St Thérèse, donated by her sisters at Lisieux, with which the crowd were blessed. For several years the event concluded with a display of fireworks, but this was later stopped because it was felt that some people were only attending for the 'show'.

The Rosary Sunday procession was led by a young 'living Madonna', regal in her blue velvet cloak with ermine trim (**37**), escorted by page boys, and girls from the Children of Mary in blue gowns and white veils. Following them were girls invited from three Catholic orphanages, holding ribbons to symbolise the fifteen decades of the Rosary – 5 x 10 white ribbons for the Joyful Mysteries, the same with crimson ribbons for the Sorrowful, and the same again with gold for the Glorious: including those holding the poles, 165 girls took part in all. Photo **38** shows part of one such procession.

38

Over the years, taking part in events like these must have left generations of children with precious life-long memories; the impact upon them would be hard to exaggerate.

43

In 1931 the Carfin Lourdes Grotto was completely reshaped, by enlarging the hill on which Mary stands (the 'Massabielle') and replacing the old slag 'rocks'. Some of the new rocks were of Westmoreland sandstone; others were man-made by a team of workers under Grotto foreman Hugh Devlin, who had devised a method of creating excellent imitations. The reshaped shrine now looked essentially as it does today (**39**).

The veneration of relics had been suppressed in Scotland at the Reformation and had died out long since. But Fr Taylor had revived this 'Continental' tradition at Carfin. For some years he had been acquiring relics and by now the parish held an outstanding collection. Since 1928 it had been the tradition to hold an annual Procession of Relics at the Grotto, using several of the most precious items. Photo **40** shows the procession, possibly from 1931. At its head is carried the relic of Our Lady, a fragment from her veil held at Chartres. Further back is the relic of the True Cross, gifted to the Grotto from Oulton Abbey that year.

At these processions it became a happy practice to invite visiting pilgrims to carry some of the reliquaries.

"HAIL HOLY CROSS"
"OUR ONLY HOPE."

The Reliquary of the True Cross (41) was the work of the Dupon family, as were most of Carfin's reliquaries.

The tradition was soon established of holding an annual Procession of the True Cross alone, so precious was the relic. The procession always concluded with a liturgy in front of Calvary Hill (42).

Considering the great number of Scottish Catholics who trace their origins to Ireland, it was only natural that the Grotto should include a shrine to St Patrick. His statue had been erected in 1930, when it was unveiled by the Belfast MP Joe Devlin. Now four years later a second item was added beside the shrine – a 'Mass Rock' some 2.5 tons in weight, donated by a Protestant landowner from Rathfriland, Co. Down, on whose land it had stood.

The Rock commemorates Ireland's Penal era, when the Catholic faith was outlawed and the Mass could only be celebrated in secret. In many country parts the people would gather for services at a 'Mass Rock', a large flat-topped stone that served for an altar.

Photo **43** from 1934 shows Fr Taylor blessing the Rock (covered with a cloth); **44** was taken some years later, when the site had been beautified with plants and the trees in the background had matured. Strangely, some four decades would pass before Scotland's own patron St Andrew made his overdue appearance at the Grotto (see page 86).

In 1934, the 19th century Italian priest and educator John Bosco was canonised. Famed for his work with disadvantaged youngsters, his canonisation was a great joy to Fr Taylor, himself so deeply committed to the spiritual welfare of the young, and arrangements were begun at once for a shrine to the new saint at the Grotto. Appropriately, the group statue had John Bosco himself with two of his young protégés, Saint Dominic Savio, and a boy whom he had saved and who later became Cardinal Cagliero. The shrine, approached by impressive flights of steps, was blessed on Palm Sunday 1935 (**45**).

45

46

That year, as usual, the Corpus Christi procession took place in June. It was always necessary to include three separate Benedictions in order to cater for everyone, and this year the third one took place at the new shrine. Among the crowd were 500 members of the Don Bosco Guild of Catholic Teachers, while children played a leading part in the pageant – in Photograph **46** can be seen 'Knights' with crosses on their robes, 'Page Boys', and Eucharistic 'Wheat Girls' and 'Grape Girls'.

47

At the 1935 procession a new Monstrance was used for the first time (**47**). Made under the supervision of M Dupon from gold and silver gifted by the faithful, this precious object, still in use today, stands 3.5 ft tall and weighs 21 lbs. It is cruciform in shape, a design criticised by some at the time, but approved and blessed personally by Pope Pius XI. The figure of Christ is done in shaded silver, the cross in mother-of-pearl and gold. In its overall design and in its detail it identifies the Eucharist and the Sacrifice of the Cross – on it Christ appears as both Victim (by His wounds), Priest (by His vestments) and King (by His crown); the Host is at His heart, while above His head are depicted the Father, and the Spirit in the form of a dove. The whole is rich in symbolism and stunning to the eye.

When at a later date a statue of Pius X (**48**) was erected at the Grotto following his canonisation in 1954, it was sited near to that of John Bosco, since he too had been deeply committed to the spiritual welfare of the young (**49**). Later again, a shrine to St Jean Baptiste de La Salle (1651–1719), the French priest and noted educational pioneer, was added to the group, his statue similarly accompanied by children.

In 1935 the shrine of St Thérèse was again
enhanced. The ground was built up, and beautified by a 'rock' garden created by the Grotto
team. Photograph 50, taken soon after the
work was completed, shows the shrine before
the later growth of trees and bushes around it.

Image 51 provides a long-range view of the enhanced shrine. It was taken from in front of the Lourdes Grotto, whose three-stepped embankment of 1924 can be seen in the foreground, looking towards the shrine across the 'Little Flower Terrace'.

Almost from the outset events at the Grotto had been drawing extraordinary crowds. Photo **52**, from *c.*1930, shows a typically packed gathering. The participants on the upper level include members of the Third Order of St Francis (TOSF) and the Catholic Young Men's Society (CYMS), as well as children. Such crowds were maintained through the '30s, a decade of huge gatherings in Scotland when (for example) Celtic Park, Ibrox and Hampden all recorded their record attendances.

Among the well attended events were those for the Blessing of the Sick. This remained, after all, a central role at Carfin, which had begun life simply as a Lourdes Grotto and which had itself already witnessed a number of remarkable cures. In the early years, especially, the shrine had been visited by many wounded veterans of the Great War. Image **53** shows a disabled woman from Dundee being carried to the Grotto by members of her family in 1924.

The first event solely for the Blessing of the Sick was held in summer 1933. When those suffering were brought to be blessed, help was at hand, to escort them to the shrine or assist them to their places. In **54** a Scout troop are bringing disabled pilgrims in.

In 55, the sick on their pallets are waiting to be blessed, with the crowd behind them taking up every vantage point.

In 1937, a processional statue of Our Lady Health of the Sick was commissioned for use at the Blessing of the Sick liturgies (**56**). Carved in wood, it was a copy of the statue of Our Lady of the Passers-By in Bruges – another instance of Carfin's Belgian connection.

Also in 1937, the Grotto acquired a second shrine depicting Mary as helper of those who are suffering. Entitled 'Our Lady Comfort of the Afflicted', it was a beautiful copy in marble of Michelangelo's Pieta. A recently taken photograph of it appears in Image **57**. For several years the statue was sited in a new part of the Grotto known as the 'Sunken Garden', the story of which is told on the pages that follow.

58

Because of the large numbers taking part in processions it was now imperative to extend the avenues. The plan was to continue the upper avenue round the far southern perimeter of the Grotto to link up with the lower avenue, a difficult project owing to the constant risk of landslips, and which required the building of a massive retaining wall enclosing the 'sunken garden' area, and much levelling of the land. When in 1936 Carfin's Catholic school and St Anne's Church in Cadzow were demolished, enough stone became available for the wall (at £25 in total!), and building began in the spring of 1937 (**58**).

By the following year a good part of the wall around the Sunken Garden was complete, and a start had been made on extending the avenue (**59**). The photograph gives a good idea of the size of the wall, which at its highest was 35 ft and 4 ft deep at its base.

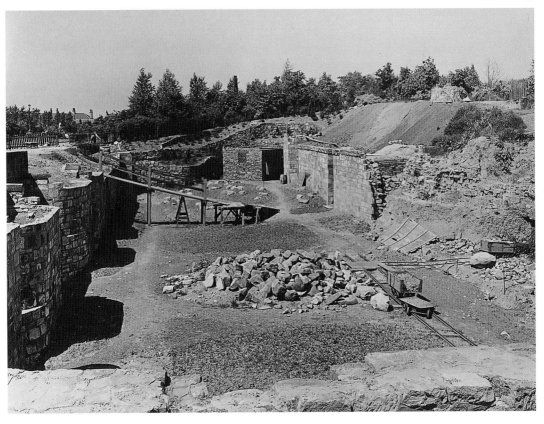

60

The work continued into 1939 (**60**), the photograph showing the progress made on the encircling avenue (dubbed 'the Miracle Road'), the wall and the Sunken Garden enclosed within it. For the workers the end of their task seemed almost in sight. But with the outbreak of war on 1 September 1939 they very soon found themselves short of manpower and without materials, and the greatest project they had ever undertaken at the Grotto was put on hold.

The war brought most things at the Grotto to a stop. Little Flower Day went ahead as usual at the beginning of October, but where 30,000 had been present the previous year, only 3000 were able to attend since there were no chartered trains, the regular services were badly disrupted, and coaches for hire were hard to come by. The events organisers bowed to the inevitable and cancelled the Procession of Relics scheduled for All Saints Day, and the rest of the 1939 Calendar. A few months later the Carfin Grotto Halt was closed. The Grotto was kept open for private devotion, and pilgrims continued to arrive on foot, often from afar. There were also visits from military and other groups, some of them from abroad. In May 1940 the Chasseurs Alpins arrived at short notice. A French élite force trained in mountain warfare, they had escaped from occupied France, and would later join the allied forces in Norway. Photo **61** shows them in procession, some bearing the canopy of the Blessed Sacrament, before which the onlookers are kneeling.

62

Goanese sailors had been visiting the Grotto annually since the '30s, and during the war they continued the tradition whenever a convoy was in port (**62**). They had a special devotion to Carfin, and to its parish of St Francis Xavier, the great missionary who had first brought the Faith to Goa in the sixteenth century and is its patron saint.

Photo 63 shows miners from the local Lithuanian community, whose families had originally come to Lanarkshire for work in the mines. Wearing their helmets, boots and working clothes, they are carrying the Grotto's near life-sized statue of St Barbara, a third century martyr who is the patron saint of miners. The statue follows tradition in depicting her along with the tower in which she was confined and wearing the martyr's crown.

On 2 September 1944, Royal Navy personnel from ships and naval establishments in the East of Scotland made a pilgrimage to Carfin, accompanied by their Chaplain Fr John Wilson. Photograph **64** shows them entering the Grotto, the procession led by two dozen Ratings (out of picture), followed by Officers carrying the Blessed Sacrament canopy, and more than fifty WRNS bringing up the rear.

With the return of peace in September 1945 it became possible to hold events again, and by the following spring the old calendar was already filling up. Photo **65** shows a dramatic detail from one of the pilgrimages held that year.

In May 1947 thousands gathered for the Silver Jubilee of the Grotto, marked with a procession led by Archbishop Donald Campbell of Glasgow, at which a large reliquary of the Little Flower was carried in public for the first time (see further page 107).

Among those taking part were 160 members of the Glasgow branch of the Catholic Transport Guild, a charitable organisation of transport workers founded in the '30s. Bus drivers from its Glasgow branch had been providing transport to the Grotto during the war, and they continued this generous work afterwards and on into the '50s. In Photograph **66**, taken in 1948, some of the members pose with Canon Taylor beside their buses.

66

Though many events had now resumed, attendances were generally down on the pre-war years. One notable exception was the pilgrimage held in honour of Our Lady of Fatima on 2 May 1948. The event was vigorously advertised, in particular by Fr Ryland Whittaker SJ, the Glasgow University Catholic chaplain, most of whose students and staff attended.

The Carfin Grotto Halt was re-opened after eight years and sixteen special trains were put on. The crowd of almost 50,000 pilgrims included virtually the entire Scottish hierarchy and 200 priests. In Photograph **67** University students have been carrying one of the processional statues on their shoulders, as can be seen by the state of their gowns.

The pilgrimage was followed by a children's pageant in the Lourdes Institute. In **68** a live 'Our Lady of Fatima' is partly hidden by the three young visionaries and others, while each of the devotees in the crowd is holding up something – perhaps one of our older readers can remember what it was?

68

70

This photograph taken of the live Our Lady on her own afterwards (**69**) gives a better view of her.

In the Marian Year 1954 a beautiful marble statue of her was carved for the Grotto by a leading Portuguese sculptor. It was set up on 'Mount Fatima', created for the purpose, along with statues of Lúcia and her cousins Francisco and Jacinta, the three shepherd children who witnessed her appearances in 1917 (**70**). The main statue was carved to a design approved for accuracy by Sr Lúcia, the last surviving visionary.

It was not until September 1951 that work on the Sunken Garden was resumed. The perimeter avenue was completed, so that it joined the lower walkway; the last stones were added to the retaining wall; and the Garden itself was cleared of rubble and laid out. For several years the team had been working on the 'Seven Dolours of Our Lady', a set of 7 ft high bas reliefs designed by M Dupon before the war, inserting them into the far (southern) end of the wall; these they now completed and painted (**71**).

Photo 72 shows the Sunken Garden today, looking north. In its far right corner can be seen a small building, the 'Holy House of Nazareth' (see overleaf).

Even before the war it had been Canon Taylor's plan to build a replica of the Holy House at the northern end of the Garden. He had sent to the local bishop in Italy for plans of the original at Loreto (which according to tradition had been miraculously transported there from Galilee), so that the replica would be authentic in every detail.

74

His team had actually made a start on the project in autumn 1939, in the first months of the war, digging the cave in the hill that had been an extension to the house at Nazareth, and building the walls of the house itself. Now twelve years on, they took up the work again, and finished it the following year. Its square exterior and domed roof (**73**), the colour of its walls, and its interior with living room and carpenter's workshop (**74**), all closely match the original.

Most of the traditional pilgrimages continued through the '50s. In Photo **75** the Legion
of Mary are walking in procession during their
annual May gathering on the feast of Our Lady
of Fatima. At the head of the procession can
be seen the Legion's standard, the Vexillum,
based on the Aquilla of a Roman Legion but
with the Dove of Peace – the Holy Spirit – replacing the Eagle of war. Our Lady's statue can
be seen in the middle ground. The Legionaries
are reciting the Rosary as they walk (compare
this image with that on page 118).

Photo 76 has captured part of a procession of the Third Order of St Francis (TOSF). Its members are dressed in their brown habits tied with a cord, which they always wore on formal or public occasions at this date, and which many chose to be buried in. At the time that this photograph was taken Canon Taylor had himself been a member of the TOSF for some sixty years. Today the organisation is known as the Secular Franciscan Order (OFS).

76

In Image 77, Mass is being celebrated for the Catholic Young Men's Society, with St Francis Xavier's Church and chapel-house across the road in the background. The open-air service is the climax of the CYMS's annual pilgrimage, and the celebrant is facing the congregation to give the homily. The triple niche with the central altar in the perimeter wall where the Mass is being held was one of the earliest additions to the Grotto, dating from 1924, and has served a number of different functions over the years.

Such events as these, and indeed the very existence of the Grotto itself, were only possible
because of the unseen work of scores of volunteers – groundsmen and gardeners, clean-
ers, caterers, stewards and many more. Canon
Taylor used to say that his faithful company
of voluntary workers were 'one of the won-
ders of Carfin'. In **78** a smiling group of young
men and women helpers from the '50s have
stopped work to have their picture taken. Today, volunteers still have an important part to
play.

In 1962 Cardinal Tien Ken Sin, the exiled Archbishop of Peking (Beijing), flew in to Scotland from Rome. He came, he said, to ask the prayers of the people for the persecuted Catholics of China. The 200,000 faithful who remained were suffering gravely. The Church had lost everything, and all foreign missionaries had been expelled. To add to their trials, the whole country was in the grip of famine.

While in Scotland, China's first native cardinal took the opportunity to meet his old friend Mgr Taylor at the Grotto. Their meeting brought together two men who were in many ways alike: both old and now almost blind, who in their different ways were essentially missionaries, and who had given all for the Faith. Their mutual respect and affection were obvious when they met (**79**).

On 1 December 1963, Mgr Taylor died, in the ninetieth year of his life and the sixty-seventh of his priesthood. His expressed wish to be buried in the Grotto could not be granted; instead, his coffin was brought into the grounds (80). As reported in the Catholic press, it was carried round all the shrines, where each saint in turn was asked to intercede for him, 'to speed his soul to heaven'. His body was then driven to the plot for diocesan clergy at St Patrick's cemetery in New Stevenston for burial.

Plaques were later mounted in the Grotto, commemorating him as its founder and giving brief details of his life, but – just as he would have wished – making no mention of his immense contribution to it, and indeed to the Catholic Faith in Scotland and beyond.

80

Two years after his death, Canon Mullen was appointed his successor as parish priest and Guardian of the Grotto. The chief project of the Canon's early years at Carfin, indeed the principal task that he had been charged with when appointed, was the building of a new parish church, since the existing building was threatened with subsidence.

The architect Charles Gray was engaged to design a building that would suitably serve both the parish and the Grotto, and the hope was that it would be completed in time for the latter's Golden Jubilee in 1972. It narrowly missed the deadline, but was ready for use and formally blessed by Cardinal Gray the following year.

The striking circular building (**81**) resembled a nomad's tent, and this was appropriate, Canon Mullen explained: Mgr Taylor had dreamed of a majestic basilica, but the post-Vatican II Church wished to stress the Scriptural concept of God pitching His tent among us. The architect's explanation was more practical – the circular shape gave everyone an uninterrupted view and allowed for processions to circumambulate the church, the roof offered good acoustics, the rows of windows made the interior light and welcoming (**82**), and the whole harmonized with the local neighbourhood.

At the same time Canon Mullen oversaw the building of a new presbytery beside the church, as well as a Parish Hall to replace the old Institute that had suffered subsidence due to underground mine workings.

The old chapel-house and the rest of the property on the north side of the road were now taken over by the Holy Ghost Fathers.

ST. MARGARET

ST.ANDREW: PATRON SAINT OF SCOTLAND
PRAY FOR US

83

84

There had been a shrine to St Margaret of Scotland (**83**) since Mgr Taylor's time, and in 1969 Canon Mullen had added close by it a statue of St Andrew, thus remedying a notable omission. An imposing work, 10ft in height and weighing 3.5 tons (**84**), its arrival was to be the beginning of two decades of new national shrines being opened at the Grotto – national shrines both of the native Scots and of Scots from ethnic minority communities.

Since 1930, the Catholic Church had been organising an annual pilgrimage to Dunfermline in honour of St Margaret. In 1975 the event was held for the first time at Carfin. The following year the Scottish martyr John Ogilvie was canonised, and as often happens at Carfin, canonisation was soon followed by a shrine to the new saint. The life-sized statue in Carrara marble (85) was erected close to that of St Margaret and blessed in July 1981. Thereafter, the practice began of holding a National Pilgrimage at the Grotto in honour of each saint on alternate years, a tradition that continues today (see one such on pages 104–5).

ON THE THIRTIETH ANNIVERSARY
OF THE EXODUS
FROM THEIR HOMELAND
THE UKRAINIANS IN SCOTLAND
DEDICATE THIS MEMORIAL
TO THE SUFFERING CHURCH
OF CHRIST IN UKRAINE
THEIR BROTHERS AND SISTERS
STRUGGLING FOR RELIGIOUS
AND NATIONAL RIGHTS
AND ALL WHO SACRIFICED
THEIR LIVES FOR CHRIST
AND THE FREEDOM OF UKRAINE

1947 - 1977

В ТРИДЦЯТУ РІЧНИЦЮ
ВИХОДУ З БАТЬКІВЩИНИ
УКРАЇНЦІ В ШОТЛАНДІЇ
ПРИСВЯЧУЮТЬ ЦЕЙ ПАМ'ЯТНИК
ТЕРПЛЯЧІЙ ХРИСТОВІЙ ЦЕРКВІ
НА УКРАЇНІ
УСІМ БРАТАМ І СЕСТРАМ,
ЩО БОРЯТЬСЯ ЗА РЕЛІГІЙНІ
І НАЦІОНАЛЬНІ ПРАВА
ТА ВСІМ, ЩО ВІДДАЛИ
СВОЄ ЖИТТЯ ЗА ХРИСТА
І ВОЛЮ УКРАЇНИ

The first of the ethnic minority Scots communities to open a national shrine at the Grotto were the Ukrainians. The Eastern Rite Catholics of Ukraine suffered severe persecution under Soviet rule, with numerous martyrs and the confiscation of all churches. In 1947 many had fled the country, some finding their way to Scotland. Thirty years later the Ukrainian Scots set up a shrine commemorating the exodus, the martyrs, and those still suffering in the homeland (**86**). The centrepiece of the triptych depicts a Church in chains; the side panels tell the story in Ukrainian and English. The shrine was opened by Bishop Thomson in May 1978, during a 'Pilgrimage of Crosses' attended also by members of the Polish and Lithuanian communities, as well as by Fr Werenfried van Straaten, the founder of the charity Aid to the Church in Need, whose main work at this time was supporting persecuted Christians behind the Iron Curtain.

87

Many Poles had served in the Allied forces in Scotland during the Second World War, and some had settled here afterwards. In 1982 they opened a shrine at the Grotto in honour of Our Lady of Czestochowa (**87**), exactly 600 years after the original. After four years of planning and raising the £9000 required, it had been built in only two weeks. The following April it was blessed by Cardinal Rubin, the Rome-based bishop of the Poles in Exile.

89

90

The Lithuanians are the longest established of these ethnic communities, and for many years have had a thriving Community Centre in nearby Mossend. Their then Chaplain Fr Petrauskas was one of the priests present at the Grotto's opening in 1922, and they had been holding their own events there since the mid-'20s. In 1985 they mounted a modest shrine there, a crucifix fashioned in the style of such wayside shrines in rural Lithuania (**88**). It commemorates Fr Josef Gatauskas who was Chaplain to the Lithuanian community in Scotland for forty years.

In **1989**, to mark the end of the Marian Year, they erected a handsome shrine to Mary (**89**), done in engraved glass and based on the icon of Our Lady at the 'Aušros Vartai' (Gate of Dawn) in the Lithuanian capital Vilnius. Mary, the gate through whom a new day dawned upon the world.

The following year Lithuania gained independence, and in celebration the community in Scotland added a third item to their shrine, a statue of St Casimir, the nation's patron saint (**90**). Like the others, it is 'housed' in the traditional national style.

One of the many appealing features in the Glasgow Garden Festival, which ran from April–September 1988, was its Glass Chapel. When the Festival closed the organising committee hoped that the chapel could continue in use somewhere as a place of worship. Here was an opportunity for the Grotto – an attractive building that could be sited actually within the grounds. Parish priest and Grotto Guardian Fr Logue was a strong promoter of Eucharistic adoration, and he saw the chapel as ideal for that purpose. He did not hesitate to find the £12,000 to bring it to Carfin, where it was re-assembled by voluntary labour.

92

The intention was for it to replace the Stella Maris shrine (**91**) and to dedicate it to Our Lady Star of the Sea, thus continuing the Stella Maris devotion (see pages 32–3). But that December, while it was being erected, Pan Am Flight 103 'Maid of the Seas' came down over Lockerbie, leaving 270 people dead. In memory of the tragedy the Chapel (**92**) was renamed 'Our Lady Maid of the Seas', with plaques mounted within recording the names of the victims. It was blessed by Bishop Devine in an ecumenical service in June 1989, attended by Fr Keegans the parish priest of Lockerbie and members of his congregation who had lost family members.

The Chapel at once became a key facility and centre of attraction at the Grotto – different, modern, drawing the visitor's eye. It was small and intimate enough for private prayer, yet also able to house public liturgies, such as this Mass from the mid-'90s concelebrated by Cardinal Winning (**93**). In the photograph, part of the congregation, seated in front of the chapel, can be seen reflected in its glass walls.

In June 1996 the Scots Ukrainian community celebrated the 400th anniversary of the Union of Brest, which brought the Greek Catholic Church of Ukraine into communion with Rome. Photograph **94**, taken during the service of thanksgiving at the Grotto, shows Canon Mykola Matyczak, with his bishop, Archbishop O'Brien and two of the congregation in national dress.

95

96

The long-felt need for a Visitor Centre at the Grotto – providing hospitality, museum, shop and parking – was finally met in 1996. The attractive building (**95**), conveniently sited beside the Entrance, was joint-funded by the Diocese, N. Lanarkshire Council, the Lanarkshire Development Agency and the Strathclyde European Partnership.

This photograph of the café area (**96**) was taken in summer 1996, just after the Centre opened to visitors. The official opening, by Cardinal Winning, took place in June 1997.

97

98

In the same year young Motherwell artist Brian Love, a former pupil of the local Taylor High School, was commissioned to paint a portrait of Mgr Taylor for the Centre. His work, based on a photograph taken on the Diamond Jubilee of the Monsignor's ordination, was unveiled by Bishop Devine accompanied by the artist and officials (**97**).

A second artwork, a stained-glass panel on the theme of 'Pilgrimage' in religions, was created for the Centre's museum by Shona McInnes (**98**).

From 1937–73 the Grotto's ever growing collection of relics and reliquaries had been kept on display in the handsome oak-panelled 'Chapel of All Saints' behind the presbytery (Image **99** gives an overall view of the Chapel; **100** shows just a few of the smaller items). Not every item was a reliquary. Indeed, as can be seen from **99**, it was the Grotto's Monstrance and Canopy that formed the centrepiece of the room. The Monstrance (see page 52) had been paid for by donations. After its purchase in 1935 enough money remained to commission a Canopy also. The task of creating the latter was taken on by Albrecht d'Harve, a brilliant apprentice employed at the Dupon Workshop in Bruges. He fashioned the panels from tulip tree wood, creating a wonderful, intricate pictorial effect; the paintwork was undertaken by Mme Dupon. The finished result was remarkable (see image **103** overleaf) – like the Monstrance itself, the Canopy is one of the glories of Carfin.

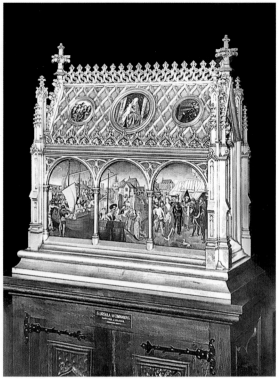

When the parish vacated the whole property in 1973 and moved across the road, the collection was brought over to the Grotto. The building now used to store the items was far too small to permit their display, so that for many years the remarkable collection with its many items of beauty – two of which are shown in **101** and **102** above – was hardly ever seen. The canopy itself (**103**) was dismantled and packed away.

Finally, in 1998 a new more spacious and becoming home, the 'All Saints Reliquary Chapel', was built beside the church, enabling the collection to be displayed and admired again. It was blessed and opened that September by Bishop Devine, pictured here (**104**) with parish priest Fr Kelly and the team who had brought it about.

103

104

In 2001 a memorial was erected at the Grotto recalling An Gorta Mór, the Irish 'Great Hunger' of the 1840s that left over a million dead and as many again forced to emigrate. The plaque tells this story, and remembers the thousands who made their way to Scotland. It was set up beside the Mass Rock and the statue of St Patrick (see pages 48–9). A Celtic cross was added in June that year, when the memorial (105) was unveiled by the Irish Taoiseach Bertie Aherne.

In the same year a statue of Pope John Paul II was erected beside the Polish shrine (**106**). The striking work by Tom Allan depicts the pope in old age, bent and ailing yet still exuding a force, still on a mission. The only statue in the Grotto to be put up during the subject's lifetime, it was blessed by Polish Archbishop Szczepak Wesoly.

107

In 2002 Fr Millar was appointed parish priest and Guardian at Carfin. During his nine years in the post he undertook much renovation work in the Grotto. His largest single project, however, was the construction of a new Hall, the 'Xavier Centre', to replace the flat-roofed, problem-plagued '70s building. The fine new facility, modern and beautifully appointed, included a large hall/café (107), kitchen and meeting rooms. Its north-west facing side was all glass, affording a panorama of the Lourdes Grotto and allowing overspill groups and others to enjoy a sheltered view of its events. The Centre was opened in 2008.

108

109

For a quarter century the annual National Pilgrimage had been the premier event of the Grotto calendar – a pilgrimage for everyone. Photo **108** from 2008 shows part of the crowd gathered for the main liturgy at the Glass Chapel; others are on the grass bank out of picture.

The rest of the season was filled with events for particular groups, such as the Polish community (see page 115), the Legion of Mary (page 118), and the Knights of St Columba, pictured here in 2009 (**109**). Since the time of the Banned Procession of 1924 the KSC have always supported the Grotto in many ways, and have often acted as stewards at events. The 2009 pilgrimage was their twenty-first, and also marked the ninetieth anniversary of their presence in Glasgow and the eightieth of their first Carfin rally.

Until 1988 the Miriam Chapel on the hill (**110**) had been the Grotto's main chapel, a retreat for private prayer and the place to which many processions made their way for their concluding liturgies. But with the arrival of the Glass Chapel this role had ceased, and for many years the Miriam was used as a store. In 2014 parish priest Fr McGachey had it cleared, renovated and dedicated to the Little Flower, renaming it the 'Thérèse Chapel'.

Visitors to the Thérèse chapel will find there a number of items associated with the saint, several of them unique. Most precious of all is a relic of her, one of four in the possession of the Grotto, set in a large Reliquary designed by M Dupon and crafted by Albrecht d'Harve. Though completed in 1939, war prevented the Reliquary being shipped to Scotland and it remained stored in Belgium until after the cease-fire (see also page 69).

The Reliquary's intricate 'halo' was originally silver in colour. It has since been gilded, as in image **111** above, which also gives some idea of its size and reveals the beauty of its details, including the rose on its lid which was carved from an ivory billiard ball.

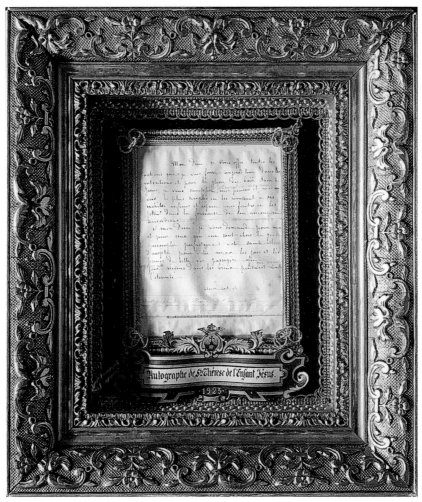

A second item, especially prized, is the saint's own Act of Consecration as a Carmelite, composed and written out by herself (**112**). This item is presently housed in the All Saints Reliquary Chapel.

LA SERVANTE DE DIEU
THÉRÈSE DE L'ENFANT JÉSUS

Image 113 shows a reproduction of the charcoal drawing of Thérèse by her sister Céline. It is said that Mgr Taylor used to pray before this portrait every day.

These two irreplaceable treasures, along with the relic, were gifted to the Grotto by Thérèse's sister Pauline (Mother Agnes of the Lisieux Carmel). Standing among them, visitors are brought very close to the life of the saint. And when they turn to admire the view of the Grotto below, they might imagine its co-patroness doing the same – looking out upon it, and watching over it.

The Thérèse Chapel was only the first of many re-openings at this time. As the Grotto had grown, upkeep had become an ever greater task, and some shrines had in time become almost impossible to maintain. Several of the enclosed or underground ones had actually been locked and put out of use long since. Now Fr McGachey made it his mission to open them to the people again, and to arrange for their upkeep once restored.

In 2015 no less than five shrines were re-opened. Two were adjacent to Mount Assisi. The Bethlehem Cave (see page 39) was renovated and given new statues (**114**), and officially opened by Bishop Joseph Toal in May.

On the other flank of Mount Assisi is the marble-clad subterranean Chapel of Our Lady of the Angels, first opened in 1931 (**115**). Based on the 'Portiuncula', the first home of the fledgling Franciscan Order in the early thirteenth century, it contains statues of St Clare, co-founder of the Franciscan Second Order, and the Curé d'Ars, one of the greatest Third Order Franciscans, as well as the Franciscan Way of the Cross. It too was re-opened to the public in 2015.

The other three re-opened shrines were in the Sunken Garden area. The Holy House of Nazareth (see pages 76–7), which had been closed for almost fifty years, was opened and blessed by Bishop Toal in June (**116**).

The other two were former shrines put to new use. The first was a cave in the wall of the Garden, long since abandoned and now restored as a Divine Mercy Chapel. The message of Divine Mercy, given by Christ to a young Polish nun, Sister (now Saint) Faustina, had been promoted by Pope John Paul II and had already become a world-wide devotion. The new chapel contains a portrait of St Faustina, as well as the familiar image of Christ the Divine Mercy.

The last of these shrines, though sited immediately above the Holy House, is actually entered from outside the Sunken Garden. Another long abandoned cave, it was re-opened as 'the Tomb of the Lord', and is one of the most arresting and haunting shrines in the Grotto. Bare and dimly lit, all the visitor sees within is the pale, supine figure of the dead Christ (**117**).

Another very recent Marian devotion that has spread widely is that of 'Our Lady Untier of Knots'. Some 300 years ago the Flemish artist Johann Schmidtner created a painting of the Virgin as 'Untier of Knots', taking the concept from an ancient Christian theme. Pope Francis, who saw the work as a young seminarian and was deeply moved by it, has encouraged the devotion, which is now widespread across the world. Its appeal, surely, is the simplicity of its message and its aptness for our lives. Late in 2015 a copy of the painting was set up in St Francis Xavier's church (118). It is hidden behind the altar screen, an appropriately 'private' place for personal petition to Mary.

The charity Aid to the Church in Need held several very well attended Youth Rallies in the Grotto at this time, where teenagers learned about, prayed for, and offered solidarity with persecuted fellow Christians. The 2017 event pictured opposite (**119**) included liturgies which united the persecuted with the suffering Christ.

Photo 120 shows the 2017 Polish pilgrimage in procession with national costumes and banners of Our Lady and the Divine Mercy.

This year also marked the centenary of the appearances of the Blessed Virgin at Fatima, in recognition of which the Church interrupted the normal biennial pattern of dedicating the Carfin National Pilgrimage alternately to St Margaret or St John Ogilvie, and instead dedicated its 2017 event on the first Sunday of September to Our Lady of Fatima (**121**).

It was a joyous and colourful day. Despite the relentless rain, some 6500 pilgrims joined seven of Scotland's bishops, eighty priests and the Motherwell Diocesan Choir for the Mass in front of the Glass Chapel, which was filmed live by Shalom TV, EWTN, and Sancta Familia

Media. A large statue of Our Lady was touring Scotland at the time, and this had been brought to Carfin for the event and beautifully decorated with white and yellow roses.

The day's liturgies were led by Archbishop Tartaglia of Glasgow (pictured before the statue of Our Lady in photo **122**).

After the Mass the crowd formed for the Rosary Procession, carrying the Grotto's own processional statue of Mary (photographs of which can be seen on pages 78 and 118).

In the course of the pilgrimage the bishops consecrated Scotland to the Immaculate Heart of Mary.

In Image 123 the Legion of Mary lead the procession in honour of Our Lady of Fatima on her feast day in May 2018, carrying the statue of her that had first been carried exactly seventy years before (see page 70). Compare this image with the one on page 78 from the 1950s. 2018 marked the ninetieth anniversary of the Legion in Scotland. The organisation has had a long association with Carfin, with a parish Praesidium founded in 1930, whose members for many years undertook the catering for pilgrims at the Lourdes Institute.

124

For well over two centuries from 1560 the Catholic Church was outlawed in Scotland: anyone practising the Faith faced punishment, and its priests were forced to carry out their work in secret (several Mass Rocks, similar to those in Ireland, have been found in the Highlands from this period). For part of the time the little clandestine seminary at Scalan, hidden high in the Banffshire hills, played a key part in keeping the struggling Faith alive. The building still exists, and re-mains as the most important *lieu de mémoire* of the Penal era that we have and an evocative symbol of a courageous persecuted people.

In autumn 2019 a simple altar was built in the Sunken Garden to commemorate Scalan and all that it stands for. It was blessed by Bishop Toal on 6 October (**124**). It fills an important gap in the Grotto's record of our Scottish Catholic heritage. There will be others yet to fill.

Between 29 August–20 September of 2019, the relics of St Thérèse held at Lisieux went on tour in Scotland, visiting each of the eight dioceses. Their first destination was the Motherwell Diocese, where Carfin was the obvious choice of venue. After an all-night vigil in St Teresa's, Newarthill, they were brought in procession to St Francis Xavier's on the morning of Friday 30th, escorted by Taylor High pupils and the North Lanarkshire Schools' Pipe Band (**125**). The church and Grotto re-mained open all day from Friday – Sunday, with liturgies that included a schools' Mass, Adoration, Confessions, Rosary and the Divine Office, as well as offering the chance for individual pilgrims to approach the casket and make their petitions (**126**). The visit came to its climax at the annual National Pilgrimage on the Sunday afternoon, with Mass concelebrated by Bishop Toal (**127**), after which the Saint's casket was handed into the care of the Galloway Diocese.

Appropriately, as this story began with Our Lady of Lourdes, it has ended with St Thérèse. For in March 2020, Covid 19 brought the Grotto to a halt, with all events and gatherings cancelled until further notice.

But the present Guardian Fr Grant and his team have not stood still. The Grotto remains open for individual visitors; Mass and Rosary services are live-streamed daily; and its website is being greatly extended and enhanced by Sancta Familia Media, allowing people to 'visit' and make a 'tour' of it, learn something of its history, view its treasures and enjoy the experience of its shrines, sunlit by day or floodlit by night (**128** opposite), at any time, in any weather, and from anywhere in the world.

This remains the position at the time of writing. We have now come as far as we can, therefore, in following the story of the Grotto from 1922 up to today. And perhaps we have even caught a glimpse into the Grotto of tomorrow.

How can we account for the remarkable story of the Carfin Grotto? It is not a place made sacred by a supernatural appearance; rather, it came about by human decision. Yet it has lasted for a hundred years, and still thrives today. How can we account for the extraordinary early growth, the wide fame and the longevity of something made by man in a little-known mining village far from the centres of society?

The phenomenon of Carfin very soon caught the attention of the secular press. One journalist, after witnessing a gathering there in 1923, commented with admiration on the Catholic Church's ability to 'stir the emotions and hold the allegiance of the people'. He was no doubt echoing the thoughts of many; and certainly he was expressing a truth, for Carfin did, and still does, stir our emotions and hold our allegiance. This is clear to see in the number and piety of its pilgrims, for instance, or in the thousands of men and women whose support and voluntary aid over the years have enabled it to exist.

This did not come about by chance. It was a sure instinct on the part of its founder that saw a place for a 'Scottish Lourdes' in 1922: saw that this was the right time, and that it would answer a need. It was a similar instinct that very soon multiplied the shrines in the Grotto, giving 'something for everyone' while still preserving an overarching unity. And successive Guardians have continued the practice with equal success, so that now most of us – including Scots of ethnic minority backgrounds – can find our favourite saint or devotion there.

Of great importance has been the strong visual impact of the Grotto. Its processions and pageants with their rich symbolism – the blessing of roses, the baskets of wheat and grapes, the living Madonnas - have always had the power to stir the emotions.

Its organisers very soon realised that involving the people in its workings was a sure way to hold their allegiance. From the beginning the men were involved in the actual building of it, and in its many later extensions; men, women and children were given meaningful parts in its liturgies; and sodalities and parish groups such as the Catholic Young Men's Society, the Knights of St Columba and the Legion of Mary etc were assigned tasks and given responsibilities at major events. By these means, generations of the laity have gained life-long memories and (in today's parlance) a 'sense of ownership' of the Grotto.

Lastly, its founder and his successors have always sought to make it a place of beauty – the beauty of nature with its lawns, gardens and mature trees, and also the man-made beauty of its statuary, shrines and reliquaries. The result must have been especially striking in the days of heavy industry, when it stood like a welcoming oasis in an unlovely landscape.

These are some of the happy instincts that have made the Grotto so appealing to visitors, made it 'work' and able to 'stir the emotions and hold the allegiance of the people'. But of course, the believer would say that this is only the human part of the story: that the skill and the labour have been driven by faith and love, inspired by God, at His disposal and for His glory; that the Grotto began, grew, and continues through the working of the Holy Spirit, and through the efficacy of prayer and the never failing intercession of Mary, Thérèse and the saints.

The Grotto's founder saw its work as essentially missionary – as a way of building the Faith. And just as he hoped that it would foster piety and loyalty to the Church, so he recognised that it was itself founded upon an existing local piety and loyalty. Indeed, it could not have been built in the first place, nor have continued to thrive for a hundred years, without an already devout and faithful laity.

We can never know its influence, of course. But perhaps there are some signs. One is the remarkable record of St Francis Xavier's as a nursery for religious vocations. In 1962 its Centenary Booklet noted that prior to 1919 there had been no vocations in the parish, but that in the following forty years (the Taylor years) it had produced no less than eighteen priests, and twenty-six female and four male Religious.

More broadly, surely the well-known faithfulness of the diocese is not unconnected with the Grotto in its midst. The very name carries an implication of fidelity – if you call someone a 'Carfin Catholic', people know what you mean, and that you are not referring to his or her place of origin.

When the Shrine first opened Catholics were more marginalised within Scottish society than today, but over the years they acquired a growing pride and self-esteem. There were many reasons for this new confidence within a changing Scottish society, but one of them was certainly the Grotto: its huge gatherings could not but give the people a great pride in their Faith.

The old hostilities to Catholicism, though by no means dead, are now a good deal abated. As to the Grotto, which met with some opposition in the early years, one would like to hope that its existence is now accepted by most in the wider community, who cannot but respect the evident sincerity of faith and the piety of those who go to pray there.

Its most newsworthy events, those which most caught the public attention, were the recorded healings, the cures of victims of severe ailments including rheumatoid arthritis, blindness, infantile paralysis, deafness, tubercular ulcers and enteritis, which could not be explained by medical science. These immediately spread the Grotto's fame through Scotland and beyond.

More important than them, though, have been the private healings that do not make the news – every prayer answered over the years, every favour granted; all the knots untied, quarrels mended, addictions overcome, hopes achieved, friendships restored, faith strengthened, lives turned round.

What of Carfin today and tomorrow? Even before Covid the visitor would have found it quieter now than in the early years, with usually just a scattering of pilgrims at prayer through the day, unless at times of major gatherings, and these no longer counted in the tens of thousands. Perhaps, though, we should be impressed not so much by any decline from the Grotto's 'heyday' as by its continued strength, despite all the changes in the Church and in society over the past half-century. In normal times it still welcomes some 100,000 visitors every year, and the piety and loyalty are still there to be seen. And if its numbers are less, in other ways there is growth. Like the Church itself, the Grotto is ever putting out new shoots.

Though its greatest growth was in the time of its founder, every Guardian since has added something to it. In every decade there have been new shrines opened, and new opportunities for devotion; and in the last ten years a number of old almost forgotten shrines have re-opened. Most recently, we are seeing the emergence of the 'virtual Grotto'. Carfin is always growing. If you are visiting for the first time in a while, you are sure to find something new, and signs of change.

And yet in its essence it is unchanging. Ninety years ago Fr Taylor wrote of this Scottish Lourdes that it was 'built upon what the Immaculate asked of Bernadette: on penance and prayer'. And this remains the case. Penance and prayer – these are the essence of the message given not only at Lourdes but at all the great shrines. They have always been at the core of the teaching of the Church.

Carfin is built on them. It gives men and women opportunities for expressing and growing their faith through prayer, both private and communal. And nowhere do we see this better than at the Glass Chapel, where they come for private prayer before the Blessed Sacrament throughout the day, but also gather to take part in the communal liturgies. And who knows what personal acts of penance are offered there to God by those seeking His mercy or favour?

Nor, amid the diversity of its shrines, has Carfin's prime purpose of devotion to Our Lady of Lourdes changed or diminished. It remains strong, and today the national charity HCPT as well as several of the diocesan Hospitalités, which exist to support Lourdes pilgrims, each come to the Grotto as the natural place for their annual 'Lourdes Day' gathering of members, helpers and friends.

Some who visit the Grotto may see it as nothing more than a pleasant garden of statues. Others as they enter through the 'Gateless Gateway' – gateless so as to exclude no one and welcome all – are conscious of being in a place somehow apart and special. In his book The Soul of Scotland, for example, Harry Reid writes warmly of the Grotto as 'a sanctuary set apart ... a serene and special place ... [with] an indisputable sense of peace'.

Those who profess the Catholic faith would echo his words, and add their own explanation. To them it is a place made holy by a hundred years of prayer, intercession, grace, and healing. They think of it, like the woman quoted by Mgr Taylor's biographer, as 'a spot blessed by God, a spot which God chose as a special meeting place, between Himself and those of His creatures in need of graces; a spot where Heaven seems nearer and where prayer could not fail to be heard'.

Photo Credits

Photos are copyright of their respective owners:

Hugh Buchanan 24, 39, 92
Derek Burns 29, 72, 81, 88, 105, 118
Kevin Cameron 70
Carfin Archive 1, 2, 4, 5, 6, 7, 8, 9, 10, 11, 12, 13,
  14, 15, 16, 17, 18, 19, 20, 21, 22, 23, 25, 26, 27,
  28, 30, 31, 32, 33, 34, 35, 36, 37, 38, 40, 41, 42,
  43, 44, 45, 46, 49, 50, 51, 52, 53, 54, 55, 56,
  58, 59, 60, 61, 62, 63, 65, 66, 67, 68, 69, 71, 75,
  76, 77, 78, 91, 99, 100, 101, 102
The Catholic Herald 79, 80 (Glasgow Observ-
  er) 93, 94, 96, 97, 98, 104 (Scottish Catholic
  Observer)
Thomas Davie 48, 84, 86, 87, 89, 106, 112, 121
Thomas Eadie 73, 74, 109, 116
Jim Hoey 108
Colin Hughes 47, 82, 83, 90, 103, 113
Imperial War Museum 64
Paul McSherry 85, 119, 120, 122, 123, 124, 125,
  126, 127
Office Central de Lisieux 3
Sancta Familia Media 57, 110, 111, 114, 115, 117,
  128
Moira Watts 95, 107

MUNGO

Publishing the Faith in Scotland

Eilein na h-Òige:
The Poems of Fr Allan McDonald

RONALD BLACK (ED.) | 2002

Poetry/Gaelic

> 'A priceless treasure'
> —Flourish

A Cairn of Small Stones

JOHN WATTS | 2006

Fiction/History

> 'A memorial to a forgotten people and
> the passing of their cherished traditions'
> —Flourish

Faith in Education:
The Teacher as Witness

THOMAS FITZPATRICK | 2009

Education

> 'A teacher's vademecum'
> —Open House

A Record of Generous People:
A History of the Catholic Church
in Argyll & the Isles

JOHN WATTS | 2013

History/Biography

> 'This is an important work ... thoroughly
> researched but very readable. I warmly
> recommend it'
> —Rt. Rev. Joseph Toal, Bishop of Argyll
>   & the Isles

A Priest in Gallipoli:
The War Diary of Fr Hugh Cameron

JOHN WATTS (ED.) | 2015

History/Biography

> 'A most welcome addition to the literature on the
> British army in the First World War'
> —The Innes Review

MUNGO BOOKS WITH CTS

A Novena to Saint Columba

REV. ROSS SJ CRICHTON | 2021

Devotion/Gaelic/Irish/English

> 'Aside from promoting a devotion to Colum
> Cille, it may engage more language enthusiasts
> here in Ireland with the writings of our cousins
> across the water, which though they are greatly
> appreciated by Irish poets, are largely ignored by
> ordinary readers'
> —The Irish Catholic

> 'This is an amazing booklet'
> —bookreviewsandmore.ca

For news and updates on forthcoming titles,
please visit **mungobooks.co.uk**

Published in the United Kingdom
by Mungo Books

info@mungobooks.co.uk
mungobooks.co.uk

© John Watts 2022
Images © credited owners
Design & layout © Mungo Books

Database right Mungo Books

ISBN 978-1-914504-00-6

A catalogue record for this book is
available from the British Library

Designed & typeset by halfapica.com
Printed by J. Thomson Colour Printers Ltd,
Glasgow